Explore (

A Geography Explorer Book

by
Mandi Watts

About This Book

The Geography Explorer Books are perfect for students seeking to supplement an existing Geography or Social Studies program, people interested in furthering their geographic educations, and travelers preparing for a trip. Though the books are geared toward students in elementary school, they can be used and enjoyed by learners of any age. The exercises and activities in this particular book are designed to help users learn more about the culture and geography of China and to act as a springboard for possible further exploration.

ISBN: 153298684X

Where in the World is China?

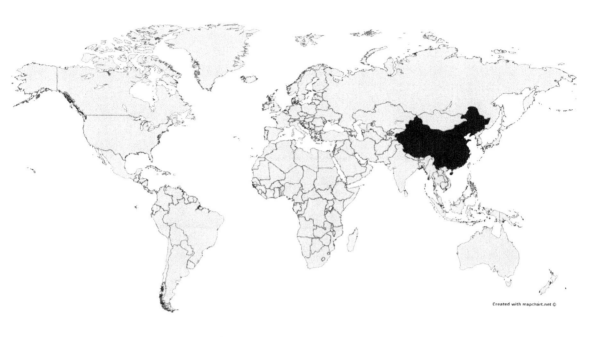

China is the world's second-largest country by land area and occupies much of the continent of Asia.

Color the Flag

Every country's flag is unique, and most flag designs incorporate a fair amount of symbolism to demonstrate ideas and traditions important to the nation flying it.

China's flag displays five yellow stars on a red field. The large star represents the Communist Party, and the four small stars represent the four social classes of traditional Chinese society. Color the flag below. If you want to see an example of the flag in color, you can find it on the back cover of this book.

coloringpanda.com

Trace China

A map of China appears on the next page. Use this page to trace the outline of the country. Be sure to label the capital city, Beijing. If the outline appears too light to trace through the paper, first trace it with a fine tipped black pen or marker on the map page.

Map of China

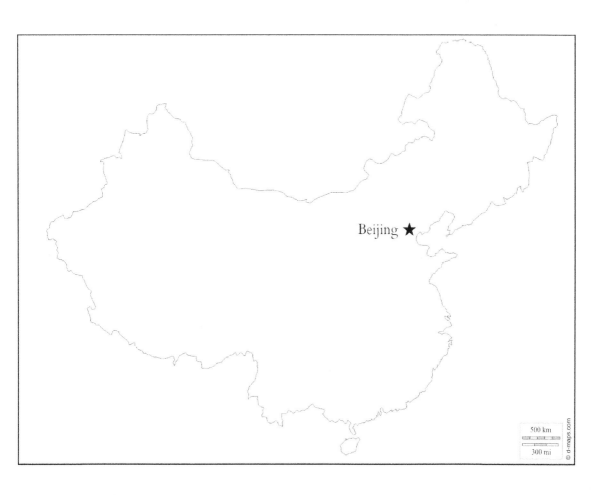

Take Another Look

Take another look at the map of China, and complete the exercise on the following page.

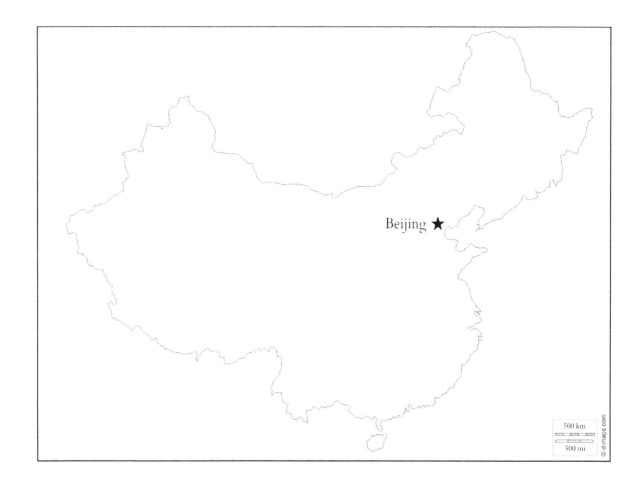

500 km

300 mi

© d-maps.com

Beijing ★

Draw China

Study the outline of China on the adjacent page. Think about where you see straight lines and where you see curves. Consider the overall shape. Now, try to replicate what you see, working in small sections. Your goal is not perfection, but rather approximation. Be sure to label the capital.

Language

The main language spoken in China is Mandarin, though there are many other languages and dialects used as well. Mandarin is a symbol-based language, using symbols to stand for words and sounds. All together, there are around 50,000 characters, but most Chinese people only use between 3,000 and 8,000 on a daily basis. Pinyin is the system used to transcribe the Chinese characters into Latin characters. The chart on the following page shows both the simplified Mandarin characters, as well as the Pinyin translation. Study the characters below, and see if you can locate them on the chart to find out what they mean.

Chinese Words and Phrases

English	Simplified Mandarin Chinese	Pinyin
Hello	你好	Nǐ hǎo
Good-bye	再见	Zàijiàn
Please	请	Qǐng
Thank you	谢谢	Xièxiè
Yes	是	Shì
No	没有	Méiyǒu
I'm sorry	对不起	Duìbùqǐ
Nice to meet you	很高兴见到你	Hěn gāoxìng jiàn dào nǐ
Toilet	厕所	Cèsuǒ
Help	帮帮我	Bāng bāng wǒ
One	一	Yī
Two	二	Èr
Three	三	Sān
Four	四	Sì
Five	五	Wǔ

*Translations provided by Google Translate

Did you notice that the symbols from the previous page mean "Hello?"

Interesting Facts about China

- The official name of the country is The People's Republic of China.

- China is the world's most populous country, with around 1.38 billion citizens.

- The currency in China is called Yuan Renminbi, and the symbol looks like this: ¥. At the time of this writing, the exchange rate is 6.48 Yuan to 1 U.S. Dollar.

- China's most famous native animal is the giant panda bear. Unfortunately, panda bears are considered an endangered species, because there are not many of them left in the wild.

- One of China's most famous landmarks is the The Great Wall. Construction on it began around 220 BC and was continued on and off for close to 2000 years. Some archeological surveys estimate the wall to have once been about 13,000 miles (21,000 kilometers) long, including all its branches.

- China is home to the Yangtze River, which is the longest river in Asia and the third-longest river in the world.

- The capital city is Beijing, but the city with the largest population is Shanghai.

- Chopsticks were invented over 5,000 years ago but were originally used for cooking rather than eating.

- Crickets are popular pets. Some are kept for their singing voices, and others are kept for fighting. There are whole pet stores in China that sell nothing but crickets and cricket cages.

- The Chinese New Year, also known as the Spring Festival, is celebrated for 15 days, around the end of January and beginning of February. Each year is represented by one of twelve animals.

China Word Search

```
E D T T P Z B K B R A C W C Y
R C B R N F I L U D C V A T A
N V I P A N D A O K W W L X N
D O B R I M I G S S P W L I G
I B G H S N A R X R A B A M T
Z K E A C P Z F A R S H K B Z
N X I I R F E V R D G D L S E
A J J Q J D P I L N N D I T R
I N A U Y I O C A F E A S E Q
J H V B I R N H H R Q O M K Y
Y F R Z Q W S G Y I Y T A C U
Q R Y T S A N Y D H N S I I V
S K C I T S P O H C I A X R O
B U D D H I S M V A N I E C U
K R H E P N X D R U S V D Y C
```

ASIA	PAGODA
BEIJING	PANDA
BUDDHISM	RED
CHINA	RICE
CHOPSTICKS	SHANGHAI
CRICKETS	SILK
DRAGON	WALL
DYNASTY	WARRIOR
JIANZI	YANGTZE
MANDARIN	YUAN

Words may be found going forward, backward, up, down, or diagonally. Sometimes letters from different words overlap.

Giant Panda Bears

Some of China's most famous native inhabitants are the giant panda bears, which live near the Yangtze River. Unfortunately, they have become endangered, and scientists estimate there are only between 1,000 and 1,500 left in the wild. Officially, pandas are considered omnivores, which means they eat meat and plants. In practice, however, bamboo makes up about 99% of the panda's diet, and panda bears munch on it for around 12 hours every day.

© Mandi Watts

A panda in the Beijing Zoo, munching on bamboo

Terracotta Warriors

Near the city of Xi'an, there is an army unlike any other. It is an army, 8,000 strong, made entirely of terracotta (the same material many flower pots are made of)! It took about 37 years to produce the life-size men and horses contained in this army, which diligently stands guard over the tomb of the first emperor of China, Qin Shi Huang. (Qin is pronounced "Chin" and is thought to be the origin of the name of the country.) Each soldier has a distinctive facial expression and a particular military rank and occupation. The army remained hidden underground for about 2,000 years, until workers accidentally discovered it in 1974, while attempting to dig a well. Archeologists are still unearthing soldiers to this very day.

© Mandi Watts

A small portion of the terracotta army, near Xi'an

Make a Chinese Jianzi Shuttlecock[±]

Jianzi is similar to hacky sack and is suitable for playing alone or in a group. It is played by kicking a shuttlecock and trying to keep it from touching the ground. No hands allowed! Jianzi is popular with both children and adults, and parks in China are full of players of all ages on weekends. New players are always welcome. Now, you can make your own Jianzi shuttlecock. When you are done, take it to the park and invite new friends to play with you.

What you need:

- 3-4 craft or bird feathers
- 1-2 Chinese coins* or washers
- Dark colored marker or pen
- Cardboard, thick plastic, or heavy paper
- A hole punch
- Strong bonding glue
- Tape or string

What you do:

Using the marker, draw about 20 circles on the cardboard or plastic. The circles should be slightly larger than the Chinese coin or washer. Cut out the circles, and stack them together to check the thickness. Ultimately, you will need to have a stack about 1 cm thick. Cut more circles if required. Tie the feathers together with tape or string, and set aside for later.

Set aside one circle. Punch a hole in the middle of all the other circles, large enough to slip the bundle of feathers in snugly. Place some glue on the solid circle, and keep it on the bottom of the stack. Then, begin stacking the other circles on top of each other, with a little glue in between to make the shuttlecock more sturdy. Try to keep the holes aligned, and try to keep the glue from blocking them.

Place the Chinese coin or washer in the middle of the stack, without gluing. Then continue piling up the circles as before, until the stack reaches a thickness of about 1 cm. You can use more than one coin to make the shuttlecock heavier, if you want. The heavier the shuttlecock, the faster it will fall and the harder you will have to kick to keep it in the air.

Place some glue in the hole of the stack of circles, and insert the feathers. Allow the glue to dry thoroughly, and check that all parts are secure before playing with your shuttlecock.

*Chinese coins may be purchased on Amazon.com.
±Project credit: hubpages.com

Finished Jianzi Shuttlecock

Top: Chinese coin
Bottom: Cardboard circle

A boy plays Jianzi at a park in China

Quiz

See how much you've learned about China by taking this quiz. Try to answer as many questions as possible without looking back in the book. If you truly get stuck, do go back and look it up.

1. What is the capital of China? _____

2. How many stars are on the Chinese flag? _____

3. Approximately how many people live in China?_____

4. Name a popular Chinese pet: _____

5. All together, how long did construction last on the Great Wall?

_____

6. What is the main language spoken in China? _____

7. On which continent is China found? _____

8. Which endangered animal is China known for?_____

9. Name a Chinese sport similar to hacky sack: _____

10. Near which city can the terracotta warriors be seen? _____

11. What is the name of the system used to translate Chinese characters into Latin characters? _____

12. How many Mandarin characters exist? _____

Recipes

Food is a very important part of every culture. Tradition often dictates what, when, and how certain foods are eaten. And geography often determines which ingredients are available. Here are some traditional Chinese dishes for you to try. For a truly authentic experience, eat them with chopsticks. **Make sure there is an adult available to help you with the cooking and cutting.**

Chinese Chive Box
(Also known as Chinese Pancakes)

Ingredients
3 cups flour
1 cup boiling water
2 bunches of Chinese chives (7 oz. total), chopped
1-2 tablespoons minced ginger
½ pound ground pork
2 oz. Chinese vermicelli (optional)
2 egg yolks
2 teaspoons vegetable oil + 1 teaspoon
2 teaspoons salt
White pepper to taste
1 teaspoon sesame oil

Directions
Stir together flour and water until it forms a soft dough.

Let dough rest for at least half an hour, covered. (This relaxes the gluten and makes it easier to roll out.)

Soak vermicelli in hot water until soft, drain and chop into short pieces.

Combine chives, ginger, pork, vermicelli, and egg yolks in a bowl.

Heat vegetable oil in a frying pan and cook the pork mixture until pork is almost done. Remove from heat and sprinkle with sesame oil.

The dough should be ready by now. Divide dough into quarters. Work with one quarter at a time, covering the rest to prevent drying.

Roll one quarter of the dough into a rope, and divide into five equal parts. Roll each part into a ball, and roll each ball into a round about 4 inches in diameter.

Place 2 tablespoons of stuffing onto dough, and seal by folding it into a semicircle and pinching the sides together. You can optionally fold the seal over itself again.

Next, stand it up, seam side up, and flatten with the palm of your hand.

Repeat until all the dough is used up. You should have about 20 "boxes" or pancakes.

Heat 1 teaspoon of oil in a heavy frying pan until hot. Place "boxes" in pan, and fry for about 2-3 minutes per side, until golden.

You may freeze the boxes before you fry them. When you want to eat them, take out the freezer, and fry without defrosting.

http://nibbledish.com/people/Enchante/recipes/chinese-chive-box

© Mandi Watts

Chinese pancakes, at a restaurant in Xi'an

Ingredients

100 wonton wrappers
1 ¾ pounds ground pork
1 tablespoon minced fresh ginger root
4 cloves garlic, minced
2 tablespoons thinly sliced green onion
4 tablespoons soy sauce
3 tablespoons sesame oil
1 egg, beaten
5 cups finely shredded Chinese cabbage

Directions

In a large bowl, combine pork, ginger, garlic, green onion, soy sauce, sesame oil, egg, and cabbage. Stir until well mixed. Place one heaping teaspoon of the mixture into each wonton skin. Moisten edges with water, and fold edges over to form a triangle shape. Roll edges slightly to seal in filling. Set dumplings aside on a lightly floured surface until ready to cook. Steam dumplings in a covered bamboo or metal steamer for about 15 to 20 minutes. Serve immediately. Makes 100 pork dumplings.

http://recipes.wikia.com/wiki/Steamed_Chinese_Dumplings

Shi Zi Bing
(Persimmon Cakes)

Ingredients:

⅔ cup granulated sugar

½ cup walnut pieces, finely chopped

3 teaspoons rosewater

2 or 3 very ripe, large persimmons

3 cups plain flour

Vegetable oil, for shallow-frying

Directions:

To make the filling, combine the sugar and walnuts in a bowl, and stir to combine well. Add the rosewater, and set aside. Wash and peel the persimmons, remove any stones, and mash the flesh into a smooth purée. Alternatively, you may place the flesh of the fruit in the food processor and process until smooth. You will need about 2 cups of purée. Please note that the persimmon is sweet but not overly so, so you may wish to add a tablespoon or two of sugar to the purée if you have a more active sweet tooth.

Add 2 ½ cups of the flour to the purée, and stir to combine well. Add the remaining flour, a little at a time, until the dough can hold its shape. The dough will be rather sticky, almost like a paste. With floured hands, knead the dough in the bowl for 3-4 minutes, or until smooth. Then, cover the bowl with plastic wrap and set aside, at room temperature, for 30 minutes.

Place the dough on a well-floured surface and divide into 10 even pieces. Roll one piece at a time into a ball, then use your hands to flatten the ball. Using a rolling pin, roll the ball into a 4-5 in. circle, making the edges a bit thinner than the middle. Place some of the walnut filling in the middle of each circle. Pull the edges up over the filling, folding the edges and pinching them together to seal. Make sure they are returned to their flattened state before moving on.

Pour enough oil into a large, heavy-based frying pan to come at least ⅓ in. up the side, then place the pan over a low heat. Cook the cakes in batches for 20 minutes, turning once, or until golden and cooked through. Drain on paper towels, and serve warm. Makes 10 cakes.

https://www.cooked.com/uk/Antony-Suvalko/Hardie-Grant-Books/The-Real-Food-of-China/Sweets/Persimmon-cakes-recipe

In your words

You have learned so much about China! What is the most
interesting thing you learned? If you were to visit China, what would
you be most excited about seeing, doing, or eating? Could you write
a story set in China? This section is for you to write out your
thoughts about China. You may simply retell what you've learned in
this book, or you may make up a story of your own, including facts
you've learned here or through other research you have conducted.
Be sure to include a title at the beginning and a picture at the end.

Your Picture

Learn More

If you would like to learn more about China, your local library or favorite bookstore is a good place to start. There are many interesting fiction and non-fiction books about China. Below you will find just a few recommendations to help you get started.

The Day of the Dragon King, by Mary Pope Osborne, is a fun adventure story in which young siblings, Jack and Annie, are magically transported to ancient China, where they experience first-hand the building of the Great Wall and see the terracotta army Qin Shi Huang is building to stand guard over his tomb. The book is fairly accurate but does indicate that the Great Wall and Qin Shi Huang's tomb are much closer geographically than they actually are. This book is part of The Magic Tree House series.
Amazon recommends for grades 1-4.

Red Scarf Girl, by Ji-Li Jiang, is an autobiography of a girl trying to figure out who she is and where she belongs during the Cultural Revolution in China. She is forced to ask hard questions of herself and those around her, though clear, easy answers are not forthcoming. It is a difficult time period, in which many Chinese people, young and old, face many atrocities at the hands of a changing government. This book is somewhat reminiscent of Ann Frank's diary
Amazon recommends for grades 5-9.

Chu Ju's House, by Gloria Whelan, is a fictional coming-of-age story, with rich and fairly accurate cultural and geographical aspects, about a girl desperate to save her little sister and determined to make her own way in the world. Chu Ju goes against deeply held but slowly changing cultural norms and demonstrates the importance of intelligence and hard work in overcoming adverse circumstances.
Amazon recommends for ages 8-12 or grades 5-9.

Congratulations on becoming a
Geography Explorer!

You can leave a review for this book
at amzn.com/153298684X

Be sure to look for other titles in the
Geography Explorer series on
amazon.com

Going on a trip?

Don't forget to take along a copy of
Go, See, Do:
A Travel Journal for Kids

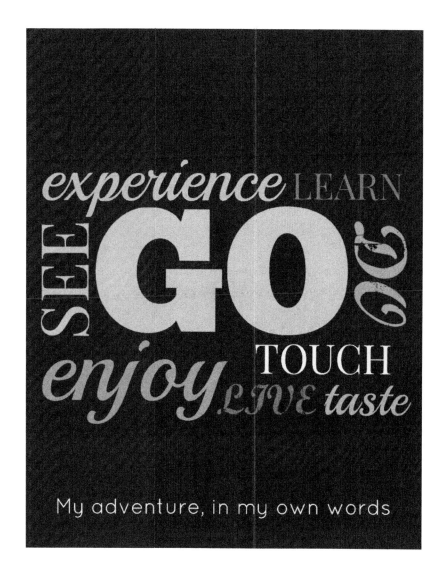

Printed in Great Britain
by Amazon